CONTENTS

HEBREWS

FAME IS SO FICKLE!

Andy Robb

Copyright © 2001 John Hunt Publishing Ltd
Text © 2001 Andy Robb
Illustrations © 2001 Andy Robb.

ISBN 1-84298- 040-8

Design by Nautilus Design, UK

Scriptures quoted from the Good News Bible published by The Bible
Societies/HarperCollins Publishers Ltd., UK,
© American Bible Society,1966, 1971, 1976, 1992.

Write to:
John Hunt Publishing Ltd
46A West Street
Alresford
Hampshire
SO24 9AU
UK

The rights of Andy Robb as author and illustrator of this work have been
asserted in accordance with the Copyright, Designs and Patents Act 1988.

A CIP catalogue record for this book is available from the British Library.

Printed in Guernsey, Channel Islands

Introduction

What's the most boring thing you can think of? Okay, now multiply it by a zillion.

That's how boring a lot of people think the Bible is. The funny thing is, most people who think the Bible's mega mind-numbingly boring have never even read it!

Crazy or what?!

Imagine turning down a triple whopper chicken, cheese and yoghurt burger with gherkin and custard relish just because you'd never tried it...

On second thoughts that wasn't such a good suggestion.

But you get my point?

I mean, I'll bet you didn't even know that the Bible's got adverts in it to tell people what's going to happen in the future or that it told people that the world was round thousands of years before we'd worked it out.

There's so much stuff in the Bible we won't be able to look at every bit of it but the bits we've chosen will hopefully make you start to realise that the Bible maybe isn't quite so boring as you thought.

Have fun!

So What's The Bible All About?

The Bible isn't just one whopping great book. It's actually 66 not-quite-so-whopping great books all whacked together like a sort of mini library.

The first book in the Bible is called Genesis, which was also the name of a pop group your parents once liked but they won't admit to it even if you hang them from the ceiling by their toenails... and the last book is called Revelation which as far as I know it wasn't the name

of a pop group your parents once liked.

To keep things simple, the Bible is mainly about two things.

God.
And people.

Some interesting questions.

Who exactly wrote the Bible?
People.

Who decided what to write about?
God.

So how did they know what God wanted them to write?
Did God send an e-mail?

Er, not quite.
Here's one way of looking at it.
Imagine two people in love.

Enough of that!
Sorry, have I put you off your lunch?
When people are in love with each other all they want to do is
spend every waking hour gazing lovingly into each other's eyes.
(I know, it's horrible, isn't it!)

The way they hug and cuddle each other you wonder whether they've been permanently super-glued to each other for all eternity.

It even gets to the point where they start to think each other's thoughts.

Well, that's sort of what it was like for the guys who wrote the Bible (without the cuddling bit).

They spent so much time with God that they got to know what he was thinking and what he wanted to say.

Sometimes God even spoke to them in dreams or gave them visions of what he wanted to say.

I THINK HIS EXCUSE THAT HE OVERSLEEPS SO THAT GOD CAN SPEAK TO HIM IN DREAMS IS WEARING A BIT THIN!

They were totally in touch with God so that what they wrote was as if God had written it himself.

So what sort of things does God want to say to us?

For starters, the Bible tells us that there is a God and that he made you and me and the whole universe.

It also tells us that he wants us to be his friends and how we can do that.

What good is a book that was written even before my mum and dad were born? People might not wear silly costumes like they did in the past but God hasn't changed a bit, so what he had to say to people with funny headdresses and sandals thousands of years ago is still important for us.

This Boring Bible book's all about a man called Abraham who travelled over a thousand miles to start a brand new nation and then all the amazing things that happened afterwards. Just like the Boring Bible book *Ballistic Beginnings*, this one's also taken out of the first book in the Bible and it's a book called **GENESIS**.

(By the way, I was only joking about hanging your parents upside down by their toenails - nose hairs work much better!!!)

In the first Boring Bible book, *Ballistic Beginnings*, we met quite a famous guy called Noah who was big in boat building.
Noah had three kids, all boys, which was great for hand-me-down clothes.

Just like when a boy band splits up and they all go their separate ways but only one of them stays in the limelight, well, that was sort of what it was like for these three boys.
It's goodbye Ham and goodbye Japheth but stick around Shem. Shem's about to be part of something even bigger and better.

Er, sorry Shem, perhaps I misled you a little.
What I meant to say is that your great, great, great, great, great, great, great grandson, Abram, is going to be a bit of a star.
Of course, it goes without saying that if it hadn't been for you, Shem, then it wouldn't have been possible and I'm sure a little of that ol'

Shem talent has rubbed off on him.
But, I'm afraid it's Abram who's our man.

Abram pops up in a book of the Bible called Genesis.
His dad was called Terah which is probably why people
sometimes called Abram a 'little Terah' when he was being
naughty!
Abram had two brothers, Nahor and Haran, and they lived in a
place called Ur.

Abram was born at roughly around 2000BC, give or take a few years.

This period of history is called the Bronze Age.

You might be forgiven for thinking that life was quite primitive 4000 years ago.

Not so!

In Abram's Babylonian homeland there were schools so that they could train secretaries to work in the local temples.

It wasn't like today when you *had* to go to school.

In those days it was voluntary.

If you didn't want to go to school then you didn't have to.

And it certainly wasn't free.

If you wanted your kids to get an education then you had to be rich.

School way back then wasn't cave painting and learning to hunt like some people seem to think it was.

Nothing of the sort.

This is how a Babylonian school week might have looked...

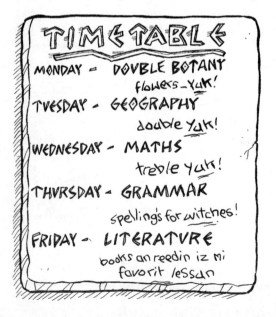

TIMETABLE

MONDAY - DOUBLE BOTANY
flowers - yuk!

TUESDAY - GEOGRAPHY
double yuk!

WEDNESDAY - MATHS
treble yuk!

THURSDAY - GRAMMAR
spellings for witches!

FRIDAY - LITERATURE
books an reedin iz mi favorit lessun

Fascinating School Facts:

Archaeological excavations have found clay tablets that show classroom exercises that the pupils had to copy. Other ones record the pupils' attempts and then the teachers' corrections.

They even had benches and desks to sit at like modern-day schools.

There was usually a professor called 'the school father' with the pupils being referred to as 'school sons'.

To make for a smooth-running establishment they usually also had a classroom assistant, some specialist teachers and others who were solely responsible for discipline.

When Abram grew up, Ur was already an ancient city.
It was also very wealthy and powerful.
It had been at its most powerful shortly before Abram was born
and was dominated by a big temple tower or ziggurat to the
moon god.
(If you've read the Boring Bible book *Ballistic Beginnings* you'll
know all about this sort of tower).
The citizens of Ur lived in well-built houses which even had
good drains which is something a lot of people who lived just a
hundred years ago didn't have.
Ur was also a centre of trade and they had dealings with people
from distant lands.

How Do We Know All Of This?

The Babylonians, like many people today, were fascinated with
history.
I'll bet even you count the wrinkles on your parents' faces to
work out how old they are.
Details of everyday life and history were written down and
stored.
The style of writing they used was called 'cuneiform script'
which is simply wedge-shaped letters that were pressed into clay

tablets.

Because clay doesn't distintegrate like paper, a lot of what they wrote has survived, which is rather handy, isn't it?

If you've ever moved home you'll know what a big thing it is.

Moving to another country is an even bigger thing.

Abram's dad, Terah, decided that they were all moving to Canaan.

'All' meant Abram and his wife Sarai, his nephew Lot and all their servants and flocks.

Why Terah decided to move the Bible doesn't tell us.

But move they did.

Ur to Canaan was no short distance.

It was a journey of roughly 1,100 miles, give or take the odd wrong turning, or 600 miles as the crow flies.

Abram's family couldn't take the direct route.
They had to follow the river to keep themselves supplied with fresh water.

THE 2000 BC HANDY GUIDE TO

TRAVELLING

① FOR STARTERS, MAKE SURE THAT THE PLACE YOU'RE GOING TO HAS ACTUALLY BEEN DISCOVERED. THE WORLD IS A BIG PLACE AND THERE'S HEAPS OF PLACES THAT NOBODY'S EVER EVEN BEEN TO.

② HAVE ALL YOUR CAMELS FULLY SERVICED PRIOR TO TRAVELLING. BREAKDOWN FACILITIES ARE A BIT THIN ON THE GROUND.

③ DON'T OVERLOAD YOUR TRANSPORT. DONKEYS ARE INCLINED TO BE STUBBORN WHEN OVER-BURDENED AND COULD EASILY END UP MAKING AN **ASS** OF YOU!

* MAXIMUM RECOMMENDED LOAD FOR A STANDARD-SIZE CAMEL IS **400** POUNDS.

* RECKON ON **10** MPD (MILES PER DAY) ON AVERAGE.

TRAVELLING HINTS 'N' TIPS

A GOOD PAIR OF WALKING SHOES SUITABLE FOR CLIMBING MOUNTAINS AND CROSSING RIVERS.

WATCH OUT FOR BANDITS, LIONS AND BEARS.

DON'T FORGET TO TRAVEL AT NIGHT - IT'LL BE MUCH COOLER. AND LAST BUT NOT LEAST, TRAVEL IN A LARGE CARAVAN FOR SAFETY!

THIS IS THE LIFE!

No, stupid. Not that sort of caravan. A large group of people travelling together-type caravan!

Road conditions:
As usual, expect little more than a dirt track that's had the trees and rocks removed. And watch out you don't get your wheels stuck in the mud when it rains.

All that remains is for us to wish you a happy journey.
Bon voyage!

Fascinating Fact:

Did you know that a camel could live for up to 50 years and, unlike trucks, they don't rust!?

As it was, they never made it to Canaan.

Terah quit when they reached Haran.

Give him the credit, Haran was still quite a trek, some 600 miles.

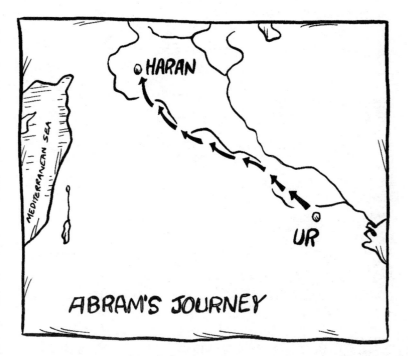

It's anyone's guess why Terah wanted to stop at Haran but one theory is that he worshipped the moon god like a lot of the folk back in Ur.

Haran was, likewise, a popular centre for moon-god worship so this could be as good a reason as any.

What we do know is that Terah didn't do any more long distance travelling.

Terah settled in Haran and eventually died there at the ripe old age of 205.

God Calling

What would you do if God spoke to you?

a Jump out of your skin?
b Think you'd heard wrong?
c Ask for a second opinion?
d Listen?

When God spoke to Abram, Abram sure listened.
Here's what God said to Abram

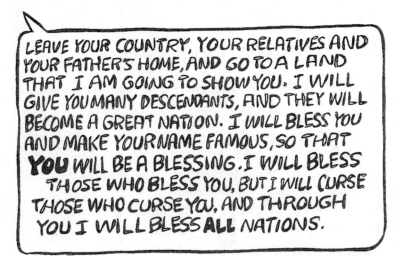

LEAVE YOUR COUNTRY, YOUR RELATIVES AND YOUR FATHER'S HOME, AND GO TO A LAND THAT I AM GOING TO SHOW YOU. I WILL GIVE YOU MANY DESCENDANTS, AND THEY WILL BECOME A GREAT NATION. I WILL BLESS YOU AND MAKE YOUR NAME FAMOUS, SO THAT **YOU** WILL BE A BLESSING. I WILL BLESS THOSE WHO BLESS YOU, BUT I WILL CURSE THOSE WHO CURSE YOU, AND THROUGH YOU I WILL BLESS **ALL** NATIONS.

Wow!

Some message.

I Choose You!

Have you ever been in a line waiting to be picked for a team at football or something like that.

When the team captain calls your name it's a brilliant feeling.

Imagine God singling you out from everyone else in the whole wide world and telling you that you'll have loads of descendants and that you'll start a brand new nation.

Hang on a minute!

Did someone say something about descendants?

Abram's wife, Sarai, isn't able to have children.

And Abram's well past it. He's 75!!!

This plan is a complete non-starter.

Forget it Abram!

Go back to Ur and live out your days.

Here's a question:

What would you do if God told you to go and do something that seemed impossible? Write down your answer.

What do you think Abram did?

No, he didn't go back to Ur.

Abram set out from Haran for Canaan with his wife, Sarai, his nephew, Lot and all the wealth and slaves they'd acquired in Haran.

How many weeks or months it took them to reach Canaan, the Bible doesn't tell us but at last they finally arrived. Hooray! They'd made it.

God even put out the welcome mat by appearing to Abram

to remind him that he was giving him the land of Canaan for his descendants.

Fascinating Fact:

Even though Abram didn't own even one little bit of Canaan, he still believed God's promise that one day his descendants would own every last inch of it!

Did You Know...?

Back in Mesopotamia, where Abraham had come from, they operated what was called a 'feudal' system for allocating the land. The king gave people some land as a gift in return for promising to serve him. The promise passed down the generations from father to son. When Abraham and Co. arrived in Canaan they brought with them the same sort of system. The only difference was that this time God was their king and he gave each family a portion of land. Each family was responsible to God for how they used the land. They didn't own it, God did.

The same plot of land would be used not only to bury your dead but also to grow your crops!

Because it was God's land, you couldn't just buy and sell the land as you pleased. And if times were hard it was the responsibility of a near relative to buy the land to keep it in the family. God had a brilliant way of making sure the rich didn't get richer at the expense of the poor. Every 50 years was a year of Jubilee. That meant if you'd had to sell off some of your land to pay a debt, the land was returned to your family in that fiftieth year. Isn't God fair?!

If you read Boring Bible book *Ballistic Beginnings*, and remember Abel and Noah, then it won't surprise you in the least what Abram did next. Abram built an altar and worshipped God. (An altar is just a stone platform

for killing animals on as a sacrifice to God.)

Because of a famine in the land, Abram and his family
wandered into Egypt for a little while.

By the time they had returned their wealth and animals had
grown greatly.

Abram and Lot now had so many sheep, goats and cattle
between them that their servants started bickering because there
wasn't enough land to graze the animals on.

Crunch Time

There was nothing for it.

They would have to go their separate ways.

Abram offered Lot any part of the land he wanted.

Hmm! The Jordan Valley looked good.

Green and fertile. Ideal!

Yep! The Jordan Valley it is.

Abram waved his nephew goodbye and Abram stayed put.

A Lot Of Trouble

The bit of land Lot chose might have looked good but the cities
of Sodom and Gomorrah that lay in the valley were terrible,
wicked places.

Good Move

On the other hand, Abram chose well.

The Bible says that God told Abram to look carefully in all directions.

All the land he could see in all directions was his for ever.

God even promised Abram that his descendants would be as numerous as the specks of dust on the earth!

That's an awful lot of people.

Leaving Ur meant a big change in lifestyle for Abram and Co.

Up till then they'd lived in nice mud and brick houses with all the mod cons.

But, if you're going to travel a long distance (or for that matter, any distance) you can hardly take your house with you, can you?

And you can't stop overnight at a hotel along the way.

Not unless you're prepared to delay your trip a few thousand years until hotels are invented.

What you need is a tent or in Abram's case, lots and lots of tents.

What sort of tent do you think Abram and his gang lived in?

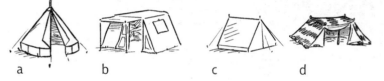

a   b   c   d

The answer is d).

How To Make A Nomad Tent

1 Weave yourself some tent material out of goats' hair. (Don't worry about it being different colours. Brown and black striped tents are all the rage.)
2 Stitch wooden rings to edge of material and also in centre. (You're going to need to put your poles through these.)
3 Prop up your goats`-hair material with poles. (The middle ones should be about six feet tall and then you'll need two outer rows of smaller poles.)
4 Finishing touches can include dividing it up into rooms with either goats'-hair cloth or reeds and twigs woven together.

A porch at the front is always nice for those warm middle-east evenings.

For that extra bit of luxury, perhaps lay a woven matting floor.

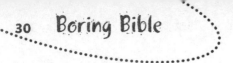

Camping in those days wasn't quite so popular as it is nowadays.

In fact, the Babylonians really looked down their noses at people who lived in tents and wandered around in search of pasture and water.

They thought that tent-dwellers were little more than savages,
eating their meat raw and not buring their dead.
(Don't worry, the raw meat they ate wasn't the dead bodies, just
in case you were wondering!)
Even today, people who move from place to place, like gypsies,
are often disliked, which seems rather unfair.
It looks like Abram gave up quite a lot to be obedient to God's
calling, doesn't it?
Let's now take a look at some of the adventures the Bible tells
us that Abram had in Canaan.

The Adventures Of Abram - Number One

'Lot nearly comes a cropper'

Four kings from Babylonia and that region went to war against
the five kings from the region Lot had settled in.
The long and short of it was that the kings of Sodom and
Gomorrah came off badly and had to do a runner which wasn't
a good idea when you end up running into a pit of tar like they
did.
The valley was full of them.

Everything and everyone in Sodom and Gomorrah was captured and taken away.

And that included Lot.

News of the defeat reached Abram so he took some fighting men and rescued his nephew. Hooray!

The Adventures Of Abram - Number Two

'Abram gets fed up waiting'

God had promised Abram that he would have a son even

though Sarai, his wife, wasn't able to have kids.

The pair of them began to doubt whether it would really happen exactly as God said, so Sarai suggested that Abram had a child with her servant-girl, Hagar.

Abram agreed and Ishmael was born.

Sarai became jealous and treated Hagar so badly that she ran away.

God saw everything that was going on and sent an angel to persuade Hagar to return, which she did.

Abram was eighty-six years old when Ishmael was born.

The Adventures Of Abram – Number Three

'New name for ninety-nine-year-old nomad'

When Abram was 99 God appeared to him with some exciting news. As Abram bowed down before God, God made a covenant with him.

(A covenant is like a two-way promise. Both sides are expected to keep their side of the bargain.)

For God's part he promised, once again, that Abram would be the ancestor of many nations.

God also changed Abram's name to 'Abraham'.

God also changed Sarai's name to 'Sarah' and once again promised to give her a son.

God promised that he would be the God of Abraham and his descendants.

For Abram's part or should I say Abraham's, God expected him and his descendants to worship him and love him.

That was their side of this special covenant.

In future years, everyone related to Abraham would also trust in Abraham's God.

Oh yes, there was just one more thing that God asked of Abraham.

I'm not quite sure how to put this.

To be honest, it's a little bit sensitive.

Okay, here goes.

God wanted Abraham to have every boy, when they were eight days old, circumcised as a sign that they belonged to God.

(If you must know, circumcision means cutting off the loose bit of skin at the end of your penis. Sounds painful, doesn't it?)

What's In A Name?

Abraham means 'father of nations'.

Sarah means 'princess'.

The Adventures Of Abram (I Mean Abraham) – Number Four

'Three angels pop in for dinner'

One mega hot day, as Abraham was sitting at the entrance to his tent, three angels paid him an unexpected visit. I guess Abraham knew that they were angels. He bowed down before them until his face was in the earth.

Abraham insisted that they stay to dinner and got Sarah busy with the cooking.

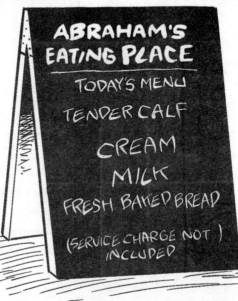

ABRAHAM'S EATING PLACE

TODAY'S MENU

TENDER CALF

CREAM

MILK

FRESH BAKED BREAD

(SERVICE CHARGE NOT INCLUDED)

While they were enjoying the meal, one of the angels asked where Sarah was.

(Only an angel would know your wife's name wthout you telling them!)

"She's in the tent," replied Abraham.

"Nine months from now, I will come back and your wife Sarah will have a son," said one of the angels.

Sarah couldn't resist eavesdropping on the conversation and burst out laughing when she heard that last bit. She reckoned that she was well past her sell-by date for having babies.

Because angels can do things we can't they knew what Sarah was thinking.

"Is anything too hard for God?" said one of the angels.

What Is An Angel?

Angel means 'a messenger'.

In the Bible an angel is a supernatural being from heaven which is where God lives.

Angels are sent by God to look after people, to give them messages from God and to do anything else God wants them to do.

Angels don't always appear as powerful, shining beings.

Sometimes they turn up looking just like ordinary people.

Nearly every time someone meets an angel in the Bible, it is so awesome that they fall down flat on their faces in fear. It is as if they were meeting face to face with God himself.

How many angels do you think there are?

a   A few?   c   Thousands?
b   Hundreds?   d   Millions?

The answer is d). The Bible says there's millions and millions of them.

The Adventures Of Abram – Number Five

'City of destruction'

Let's not beat about the bush.

When Lot chose Sodom to live in he made a bad, bad choice.

It might have looked good on the outside but, like a rotten apple, it wasn't very nice on the inside.

God told Abraham that Sodom's days were numbered.

He was going to destroy the whole stinking valley with all of its wickedness.

Abraham pleaded with God to think again.

Perhaps if there were 50 innocent people in that city, maybe then God would spare it.

God agreed to Abraham's plea.

But there weren't.

Nor were there...

No, there weren't even ten innocent people in that whole region.

Sad to say, Lot was the lot.

There were no other good people to be found.

God told Lot to get out of the city pronto and take his relatives with him.

As it was, most of them didn't take Lot seriously and it was all he could do to drag his wife and two daughters away just in the nick of time.

As soon as they were safely out of the area, God rained down burning sulphur onto the cities of Sodom and Gomorrah, destroying them completely.

Lot's wife's heart wasn't in it and she turned back and got engulfed by the terrifying rain.

Fascinating Fact:

*If you walk around the Dead Sea today,
(that's where Sodom used to be) you can pick up lumps
of sulphur and tar just like the Bible says were
in the valley.
There are also large deposits of salt in the rock.
Because the valley that Sodom was in was unstable,
it is not too hard to imagine a volcanic explosion
melting the salt, igniting the tar and sulphur then
sending it all sky high and raining it back down again
onto the inhabitants of those wicked cities.
Such was the power of the destruction that Sodom sank
into the sea and now rests 50 feet beneath the surface.
Even today you can see salt-covered trees standing there
as if caught in time as pillars of salt.
Who knows, one of them might even actually be Lot's
wife, who the Bible tells us became like a pillar of salt.*

Boy, Oh Boy!

It's party time down at Abraham's place.

After waiting a quarter of a century, Sarah's had the baby boy that God had promised them.

There's only one possible name that Abraham can call his newborn son.

It has to be Isaac.

Isaac means 'he laughs' which is precisely what Abraham did when he was told that his barren wife would have a child.

Abraham wasn't the only one to laugh at God's suggestion.

Sarah couldn't help having a snigger as well.

But God had the last laugh with this one.

The Bible, time and time again, goes on reminding us that when

God promises something he always comes up with the goods.

Abraham practised what he preached and had Isaac circumcised eight days after he was born.

Ishmael and Isaac grew up side by side but Sarah didn't like the idea of Ishmael inheriting any of Abraham's wealth.
She persuaded Abraham, much against his better nature, to send Ishmael and his mother, Hagar, away.

Fascinating Fact:

The Bible tells us that Abraham was uneasy about sending Hagar and Ishmael away.
The reason for this was that although it was acceptable by the local customs of Abraham's time to have a child by a slave-girl (if your wife couldn't have children) you weren't allowed to then send them away.

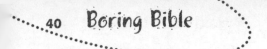
Parting Is Such Sweet Sorrow

Early next morning, with her son and a packed lunch, Hagar set out into the wilderness.

When her food was all gone she left Ishmael under a bush and prepared herself to die in the scorching desert sun.

As she wept, an angel came down to comfort her.

God promised Hagar that he would also make a great nation out of Ishmael's descendants.

The angel led Hagar to a well so that she could refill her water bag and as the boy grew up in the wilderness God was always with them and helping them.

Boring Bible Joke:
Why did Hagar and Ishmael go off?
Because Abraham didn't keep them in the fridge!

Hands up everyone who likes tests?
Me neither.
Not many of us like being put on the spot.
But don't worry, this time it's Abraham who's being tested and it's God who's doing the testing.

Abraham Of Canaan. This Is Your Moment Of Truth...

ABRAHAM!

YES, HERE I AM!

TAKE YOUR SON, YOUR ONLY SON, ISAAC, WHOM YOU LOVE SO MUCH AND GO TO THE LAND OF MORIAH. THERE ON A MOUNTAIN THAT I WILL SHOW YOU, OFFER HIM AS A SACRIFICE TO ME!

Abraham did as God commanded.

Early next morning, with his donkey loaded up with freshly cut wood for the sacrifice, with Isaac and two servants, he set out for the place God had told them. When they were a short way off, Abraham left his servants with the donkey and continued on with just Isaac and the stack of wood.

At the place God had set, Abraham built an altar and put the wood on top.

Then Abraham tied Isaac up and placed him on the altar.

Just as he lifted his knife to kill his precious son an angel from heaven called out to him...

Nearby, a ram was caught in a thorn bush.
Abraham took the animal and sacrificed it to God instead of his son, Isaac.

Phew! That was a close one!

I Hereby Certify
that...Abraham... has

passed his
"TRUSTING IN GOD"
test and because he has obeyed
God he will be richly blessed
by God and his
descendants will be as
numerous as the stars in the sky.

PASS MARK 100%
YOUR MARK 100%

Just In Case You Were Worried...

God wasn't being cruel or unkind. The Bible makes it clear that God had no intention of letting Abraham kill Isaac. What God was doing was seeing how much Abraham trusted God. After all hadn't he promised Abraham that through Isaac he would have many descendants? God had very special plans for Abraham and the nation that would come from him but it was very important that they were a nation of people who trusted God completely and who knew that everything God did for them was for their own good.

I think Abraham must have learned a whopping great big lesson that day!

Sarah Dies

At the good old age of 127, Abraham's wife, Sarah, died.

Abraham was a bright chap and he realised that sooner or later his son Isaac was going to have to have kids of his own if the great nation that God promised was ever going to happen.

R.I.P.

Here lies the body of Abraham's wife ... Up until yesterday, she was so full of life!

And what do you need if you're going to have kids? You need a wife.

Canaan, where Abraham lived, wasn't a good place to look. The people of the land didn't worship Abraham's God. Abraham needed to find Isaac a wife from his own people which meant going back to Haran in Mesopotamia.

GOD-FEARING GUY seeks
God-fearing gal.
Likes: Camping and
Mesopotamian girls.
Dislikes: Being sacrificed
and Canaanite girls.
Family Background: Originally
from Ur.

Abraham was getting on a bit and a trip to Haran was out of the question.

Instead, Abraham sent one of his trusty servants to do his detective work.

Mission (Nearly) Impossible!

Your mission: Travel to Northern Mesopotamia, to my brother Nahor's family, and find a wife for my son Isaac.

Go to a well to water your camels. When one of the young women comes to get water ask her to lower her jar to give you a drink. If she also offers you water for your camels then she is the person we are looking for. This will be taken as confirmation from God.

Abraham's servant did just that.
Even before he had finished praying to God about his mission,
Rebecca, the daughter of Abraham's brother Nahor, turned up
and offered to water the servant's camels as well as give the
servant water.

The Bible says that when the servant found out who she was he
was over the moon and praised God.
Rebecca's family could see that this was all part of God's plan so
they allowed their daughter to travel back with the servant to
Canaan where Isaac and Rebecca were married.
I love happy endings.

Believe It Or Not!

Even though he was well past 100 years old Abraham
remarried!
His new wife's name was Keturah.
Not only that but he had another six children by her!!!

Abraham still left everything he owned to Isaac but while he
was still alive he gave presents to all his new children. Wasn't he
kind?

Time Up

At the ripe old age of 175 Abraham died and was buried with his wife Sarah.

The Bible doesn't have loads of stuff about Isaac, just two or

three chapters. (Bible chapters aren't usually as long as normal book chapters.)

One thing the Bible does tell us about Isaac is that he had two sons or, more to the point, twin sons.

Double Trouble

Isaac and Rebecca were having a bit of trouble having children so they prayed to God and he answered them big time.
Rebecca became pregnant with not one child but two.
Most brothers and sisters fight some time.
But Isaac's kids must have taken the record for being the world's youngest squabblers.
They started having a go at each other while they were still in the womb!

WHY'S THIS HAPPENING TO ME?

BIFF! BASH!

TWO NATIONS ARE WITHIN YOU. YOU WILL GIVE BIRTH TO TWO RIVAL PEOPLES. ONE WILL BE STRONGER THAN THE OTHER THE ELDER WILL SERVE THE YOUNGER.

...said God.

It looks like we're in for more than just your average bit of brotherly rivalry with these two.
And what was that about the elder serving the younger?
It's usually the other way round.
I wonder what trouble's brewing?

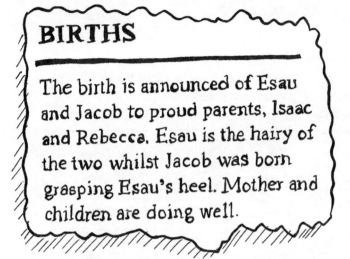

BIRTHS

The birth is announced of Esau and Jacob to proud parents, Isaac and Rebecca. Esau is the hairy of the two whilst Jacob was born grasping Esau's heel. Mother and children are doing well.

Did you know that Esau means 'hairy' and Jacob sounds like the Hebrew word for 'heel'?

Try saying this tongue twister as fast as you can.
I saw Esau sitting on the see-saw
Who saw Esau sitting on the see-saw?
'E saw Esau sitting on the see-saw.

Storytime With Esau And Jacob

Are you sitting comfortably?
Then I'll begin.
Once upon a time there were two brothers, Esau and Jacob.
Esau, the eldest son, was a skilled hunter and he loved the outdoor life.

On the other hand, Jacob, the youngest son, was a quiet man who preferred to stay at home.

Bad Move

It's never a good thing for parents to have favourites but
Isaac's favourite son was Esau because he liked eating the
animals Esau killed.

Rebecca, on the other hand, favoured Jacob.

One fine day, while Jacob was cooking up a delicious bean stew
(yummy, my favourite!), Esau returned, all grumpy and hungry.
"Who's been sleeping in my bed?" demanded Esau (Oops!
Sorry. That's the wrong story.)

"I'm starving; give me
some of that red stuff",
demanded Esau.
(Red stuff??? That's a bit
rude isn't it?)
"I'll swap you some of my
bean soup for all of your
rights as first-born son,"
said Jacob.
Esau was hungry after a
good day's hunting and
agreed to Jacob's
outrageous demands.

"Oh, all right! I'm about to die of stavation anyway so what
good will my rights do me then," snapped Esau,
over-exaggerating just a teensy bit, don't you think?
"First make a vow that you will give me your rights," said Jacob,
somewhat cunnningly.
He wasn't going to part with a few dollops of 'red stuff' just to
have his brother suddenly change his mind once his stomach
was full.

So silly Esau made the vow and gave away all his rights as the eldest son just for some bean stew (okay, admittedly it was nice, but not that nice)...and a little bit of bread which Jacob threw in for good measure.

Tricky question:

Suppose you'd had a busy day at school and hadn't eaten all day.

What would you exchange for a decent slap-up meal?

a One week's pocket money?

b Your personal stereo?

c All your birthday and Christmas presents for one year?

d Everything that your mum and dad will ever give to you?

If you answered d) then you're in good company. That's about the size of what Esau did!

Even when their dad was old, Esau and Jacob were still trying to get the better of each other.

Two-Nil To Jacob

It was the custom then, and still is, for the eldest Hebrew son to receive his father's blessing before his father died.

(A Hebrew was a descendant of Abraham and someone who belonged to the new nation that God had started through Abraham.)

A blessing really meant something to the Hebrews. They believed that as they spoke the words, God would make what they said happen.

Words were really thought to be powerful.

If you've read Boring Bible book *Ballistic Beginnings* then you'll remember that God created the entire universe just by speaking it into existence.

Before Isaac blessed Esau, he sent him out to kill an animal and cook it.

Little did frail old Isaac know that Rebecca was hovering in the wings.

She heard every word Isaac said to Esau and immediately set about a sneaky plan to dupe Isaac.

Jacob was her favourite and she wanted him to get the blessing. Isaac might have had poor eyesight but he'd have no trouble telling the two brothers apart. All he had to do was feel their skin and he'd know which was which. Esau was the hairy one. Undeterred, Rebecca flung goat skins around Jacob's neck and on his arms and then quickly cooked up a tasty meal for Isaac. Pretending to be his brother Esau, Jacob slipped into Isaac's room and then bluffed his way into getting Isaac's blessing. What a sneaky trick!

No sooner had Jacob left the room than Esau returned. Not suspecting the dirty deed that had been done while he'd been away Esau cooked his father a meal and took it in. Isaac trembled when he realised that he'd been deceived by Jacob.
Esau wept and begged his father to bless him but he couldn't. There was only one blessing to have and Jacob had tricked his way into getting it.

Esau was furious.
As soon as Isaac was dead he was going to murder Jacob. Rebecca, fearing the worst, packed Jacob off to her brother Laban back in Haran.

Guilty Or Not Guilty?

Boring Bible Poser: Who of the two do you think was most in the wrong?

"The case against Esau is as follows. In regard to his birthright, he considered it of such little value that he sold it for a bowl of stew, would you believe? A most foolish and frivolous gesture I suggest. In regard to the blessing, he has nothing to complain about whatsoever. In vowing to sell his birthright he was then breaking his oath to his brother when he begged Isaac to bless him. And, in conclusion, Esau has been unwise in the extreme by taking foreign wives who bring with them their foreign gods. This is wholly inappropriate for a descendant of Abraham."

☐ **GUILTY**

☐ **NOT GUILTY**

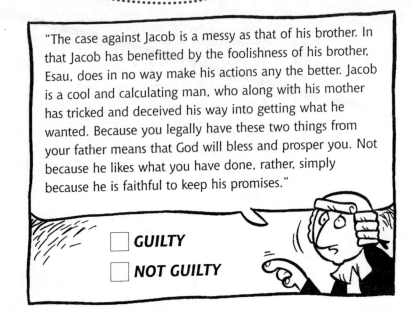

"The case against Jacob is a messy as that of his brother. In that Jacob has benefitted by the foolishness of his brother, Esau, does in no way make his actions any the better. Jacob is a cool and calculating man, who along with his mother has tricked and deceived his way into getting what he wanted. Because you legally have these two things from your father means that God will bless and prosper you. Not because he likes what you have done, rather, simply because he is faithful to keep his promises."

☐ **GUILTY**

☐ **NOT GUILTY**

Isaac's Final Blessing

Before Jacob escaped to Haran, Isaac had some things he wanted to say.

DON'T MARRY A CANAANITE GIRL. MARRY ONE OF YOUR UNCLE LABAN'S DAUGHTERS. MAY GOD BLESS YOUR MARRIAGE SO THAT YOU BECOME THE FATHER OF MANY NATIONS. MAY GOD BLESS YOU AND YOUR DESCENDANTS LIKE HE BLESSED ABRAHAM. MAY YOU POSSESS THE LAND WHICH GOD GAVE TO ABRAHAM.

And with that, Jacob took to his heels and fled to Mesopotamia.

Jacob's Dream

It was quite a trek to Haran and Jacob would spend many days on the road before he got there.

As he lay down to sleep that first night, his head resting on a stone (bet that was uncomfortable!), Jacob began to dream a most unusual dream.

Jacob dreamt that he saw a stairway reaching from earth to heaven with angels going up and down it.

And there stood God, speaking to him.

I AM THE LORD, THE GOD OF ABRAHAM AND ISAAC. I WILL GIVE TO YOU AND YOUR DESCENDANTS THIS LAND ON WHICH YOU ARE LYING. THEY WILL BE AS NUMEROUS AS THE SPECKS OF DUST ON THE EARTH. THROUGH YOU AND YOUR DESCENDANTS I WILL BLESS ALL NATIONS. REMEMBER I WILL BE WITH YOU WHEREVER YOU GO AND I WILL BRING YOU BACK TO THIS LAND.

If I were Jacob, running away in fear, then what God had just said would make me feel a lot better.

Four Things Jacob Did When He Woke Up Next Morning

1 Used his rock pillow as a memorial to what had happened.
2 Dedicated it to God by pouring olive-oil on it.
3 Named the place Bethel which means 'house of God'.
4 Promised to give God a tenth of all his wealth.

Interesting Point

Do you notice how time and again God keeps repeating his promises to the Hebrew people. I'll bet that gave them a lot of confidence in God!

LOVE AT FIRST SIGHT

At long last, Jacob's journey to Haran was almost over.

He came to a well that the local shepherds used to water their sheep.

As he was talking to the shepherd, his cousin Rachel showed.

Wow! Was she beautiful or what?!

Jacob wasted no time in introducing himself to Rachel.

Who wouldn't?

Rachel raced back home to tell her dad about Jacob.

Laban was overjoyed and welcomed Jacob with open arms.

The Bible tells us that Laban greeted Jacob with the words...

which could have meant nothing more than "you're one of my relatives".

But, as we will very soon find out, what it more likely meant was something along the lines of...

Jacob's stay with his uncle wasn't just a holiday. Jacob helped out around the place. Not wanting to take advantage of him, Laban made up his mind to pay Jacob for his work.

Love-struck Jacob wanted nothing more than the hand of Rachel in marriage as his wages.

The Bible says that it only seemed like a few days to Jacob because he loved her. All say "Aaah".

What Was Work Like Then?

As you can imagine, in those days the main job that people did was farming. Footballers, pop stars, bus drivers and mobile phone salesmen were few and far between.

People kept goats, cattle and sheep which not only gave them a slap-up Sunday roast but also nice big helpings of manure to help the crops grow.

Everything was based around the seasons. There was a wet
season and there was a dry season.

From October to April, while the rains fell, farmers prepared the
ground, sowed the seed and cleared away the weeds.

Harvest time was from April through to November yielding a
wonderful variety of crops: flax, barley, wheat, grapes, figs and
olives.

It wasn't just the men who had to work hard, the women did as
well. They couldn't just pop down to the shops to pick up a loaf
of bread. They had to make it by grinding the grain, making
dough and then baking it.

Every single day!
And you couldn't just turn on your tap for water. You had to go and collect it from the well. That was a job for the ladies as well, carrying the heavy water-jars on their shoulders.

Life on the land was very hard work indeed and there were always the unpredictable things like a drought or a swarm of crop-devouring locusts.

Seven Years Later

"Time's up", said Jacob.
"Let me marry Rachel."
Laban was as good as his word (or so it seemed!!!) and he threw a wedding feast for anyone and everyone.

Now, here's where Laban shows his true colours.
That night Laban switched the brides.
Instead of giving Rachel to Jacob, he gave him Rachel's older
(and not quite so lovely) sister, Leah.

Didn't I tell you Laban was a crook?!
Only next morning did Jacob realise that he had been tricked but then it was too late.
He was married to Leah.
What a mess!

Hang on a minute...

Was Jacob blind? Why on earth didn't he spot that it wasn't Rachel he'd married?
That's a very good question.
One possible reason could have been that Leah was wearing a veil and in the half-darkness her features were obscured.

Laban's very poor excuse for deceiving his nephew was simply that it wasn't the custom there to marry off the youngest daughter first.
He might have had the decency to tell Jacob that seven years ago!

Jacob resisted the temptation to strangle his father-in-law and agreed to work for Laban another seven years in return for Rachel in marriage.
Luckily, he didn't have to wait another seven years to actually marry Rachel.
As soon as the week of celebrations for Leah's wedding were finished, Jacob was able to marry his sweetheart, Rachel.

Fascinating Fact:

In case you're wondering, yes they were allowed to have more than one wife in those days. Having several wives had its downside though. It must have been all too easy for a husband to have favourites which would have caused lots of jealousy. And then think of the cost of all those kids! No wonder the custom eventually died out.

Let's be honest, Jacob and Leah's was hardly a marriage made in heaven.

For a start, Jacob's heart really wasn't in it and he still loved Rachel best.

But God felt sorry for Leah so he gave her some children.

They were four boys called Reuben, Simeon, Levi (nothing to do with jeans!) and Judah.

All the while Rachel remained childless.

In fact, Rachel became somewhat jealous of her sister...

Can you remember back to what Abraham did when his wife Sarah couldn't bear him any children?

That's right.

He had a son by his slave-girl.

As they say, history always seems to repeat itself and Rachel, in her jealousy and anger, told Jacob to go and have some children by her slave-girl, Bilhah.

Which he did.

Boring Bible Joke:
Did Abraham charge the slave-girl for having his baby?
I don't know but the Bible does say that he went to
BILL-HER!

The battle lines were now drawn between Rachel and Leah. Bilhah gave Rachel two sons, Dan and Naphtali.

The Score So Far

AND THE SCORES SO FAR ARE AS FOLLOWS...
AFTER TAKING AN EARLY LEAD WITH FOUR
KIDS IN QUICK SUCCESSION, LEAH'S TEAM NOW
APPEARS TO BE COMING UNDER ATTACK FROM
RACHEL'S SIDE. THE SURPRISING MID-SEASON
SIGNING OF BILHAH HAS CHANGED THEIR
FORTUNES OVERNIGHT. TWO BOYS FOR RACHEL
BRINGS HER BACK INTO THE GAME. IT'S
4-2 TO LEAH BUT EVERYTHING TO PLAY FOR.

SPORTS DESK

TV

Fascinating Fact:

The slave-girl's children would have been counted as
Rachel's own even though she didn't actually bear them.

Sports Flash

WE INTERRUPT OUR SCHEDULED SPORTS PROGRAMME TO BRING YOU THE LATEST UPDATE ON WHAT HAS COME TO BE KNOWN AS 'THE BATTLE OF THE SISTERS'. THINGS ARE HOTTING UP IN THIS LOCAL CONTEST. LEAH'S TEAM, NOT WANTING TO BE OUTDONE, HAVE PULLED IN SLAVE-GIRL ZILPAH FROM THE SUBS' BENCH, WHO'S PRODUCED A COUPLE OF CRACKING KIDS. (GAD AND ASHER) FOR JACOB. AT 6-2 TO LEAH, IT'S NOT LOOKING GOOD FOR RACHEL. WE'LL BE BACK AFTER THE BREAK.

WELCOME BACK. WE'VE BROKEN AWAY FROM OUR SCHEDULED PROGRAMMES TO GIVE YOU BALL BY BALL COMMENTARY ON THE LEAH/RACHEL MATCH. SINCE WE WENT OFF AIR, LEAH HAS ALSO GIVEN BIRTH TO TWO MORE BOYS CALLED ISSACHAR AND ZEBULUN AND A DAUGHTER, DINAH, BUT IN KEEPING WITH THE RULES OF THE GAME, WHICH IS 'BOYS ONLY', THE BIRTH HAS BEEN DISALLOWED. JUST WHEN IT LOOKED LIKE RACHEL'S OUT OF THE RUNNING SHE DOES SOME SKILLFUL PRAYING TO GOD AND GETS THE RESULT SHE'S LOOKING FOR; ANOTHER BOY, JOSEPH, BRINGS THE SCORE UP TO 8-3. WHAT A MATCH THIS IS TURNING OUT TO BE. BUT THERE GOES THE FINAL WHISTLE. IT'S A RESOUNDING WIN FOR LEAH. EIGHT SONS! CAN YOU BELIEVE IT? THIS HAS TURNED OUT TO BE A BETTER SEASON FOR LEAH THAN SHE COULD EVER HAVE IMAGINED.

SPORTS DESK

Time To Go

At long last, Jacob decided that the time was right to go back home to Canaan. All Jacob wanted from Laban was to take his wives and children as payment for the work he'd done for him. Laban had prospered all the while Jacob had been there because God had blessed Jacob just like he'd promised.

Laban insisted that Jacob be repaid for all his
hard work so Jacob asked to take every
black, spotted or speckled young goat
from among Laban's flock.

Laban agreed, but watch out, Jacob.
Remember how Laban tricked you with
his daughters. Laban couldn't even be
trusted to tell an honest lie!

I Told You So

While Jacob's back was turned, Laban
went through his entire flock and
removed all the black, spotted, striped and speckled goats.
He put his sons in charge of them and they went with them as
far from Jacob as they could get in three days.

Didn't I say that Laban couldn't be trusted?
Meanwhile, Jacob continued to look after the rest of Laban's
flock.
Fortunately, Jacob was well aware what Laban was up to. God
appeared to him in a dream and warned him. God also showed
Jacob how to outwit his scheming uncle.

The Plan

Get green branches of poplar, almond and plane trees.
Strip off some of the bark so that the branches look striped.
Place the branches in front of the flocks at the drinking troughs
(because that's where the animals mate).

The Result

When the goats breed in front of the branches they'll produce
young that are streaked, speckled and spotted.
Jocob did the same with the sheep, making sure that he only
bred strong animals, leaving Laban the weak ones, until his
flocks and herds were enormous and Laban's were weak and
sickly.

Laban's brothers were none to happy that their family wealth
was going down the pan whilst Jacob was flourishing.
Jacob could see that Laban was quickly turning against him and
God saw that as well...

> # GO BACK TO THE LAND OF YOUR FATHERS AND TO YOUR RELATIVES. I WILL BE WITH YOU.

...said God.

A Quick Getaway

While Laban was out shearing the sheep Jacob seized his opportunity to leave. Gathering together his family and flocks he made his escape.

Rachel and Leah had no problem with leaving their father. As far as they were concerned he'd treated them just as badly. He had spent the 'mohar' - the money given to him by Jacob as a bride-payment.

Rachel, thinking she was getting her own back, stole Laban's collection of idols or household gods.

She mistakenly thought that they would give her the right to some of her father's inheritance.

Gotcha!

Laban wasn't going to be outsmarted by his nephew, Jacob, so he set off after him in hot pursuit.

Ten days later Laban and his men caught up with Jacob somewhere around here...

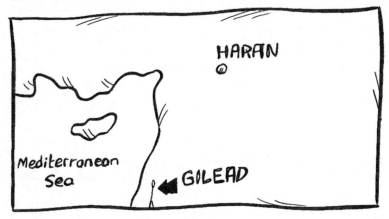

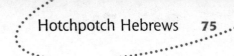

Sorry, Laban, but we don't believe you for a minute!

Things could have turned nasty if God hadn't appeared to Laban in a dream and told him to keep his hands off Jacob.

Laban hunted high and low, going in and out of every tent he could see.
But they were nowhere to be found.
I wonder if Rachel knows where they are?

Jacob had had enough of playing 'hunt the idols'.

> I'VE HAD IT UP TO HERE WITH YOU, LABAN, YOU OLD CROOK. IF YOU'D HAD **YOUR** WAY I'D HAVE COME AWAY FROM YOU EMPTY-HANDED BUT GOD HAS LOOKED AFTER ME AND BLESSED ME DESPITE ALL YOUR SCHEMING!

Laban decided to call a truce.

Laban wouldn't pursue Jacob any more if he promised to take good care of Laban's daughters and grandchildren.

The deal was sealed with a memorial built out of rocks.

So Laban and Jacob finally went their separate ways.

I Saw Esau...

Jacob knew that to return to his homeland also meant meeting his brother Esau again.

Jacob had no idea how Esau would be.

Was he still angry with Jacob for tricking him out of his birthright?

A lot of years had passed but maybe Esau had just grown angrier and angrier.

Jacob was scared.

But there was one thing the Hebrew people had learned to do in times of trouble...

What Would You Do If You Were Jacob?

a Go straight up to Esau and blow a great big raspberry in his face?

b Disguise yourself as someone else and hope he doesn't recognise you?

c Give him a little certificate which says that Esau can have his birthright back?

d Buy him a nice big bunch of flowers and hope that he doesn't suffer with hayfever?

e Cling to his ankles and beg for mercy?

f Pretend you've gone completely mad?

g Anything else?

Jacob opted for the gift approach. He picked out some of his best animals as a goodwill prezzie for his brother and sent them ahead with servants in three groups to soften Esau up.

(Jacob had already sent some men ahead to warn Esau that Jacob was on his way. Esau's reply was to come out to meet his deceiving brother...with 400 men!!!)

In final preparation for this momentous meeting with his brother, Esau, Jacob sent his wives and children across the river, ahead of him.

He needed some time alone.
The last thing he was expecting at that particular moment was a fight with God.

Seconds Away - Round One...

The Bible says that a man, or God, came and wrestled with Jacob.
It was probably an angel.

They wrestled long and hard through the night.
Jacob would not give up.
When the angel saw that he wasn't winning he struck Jacob on the hip so that it was thrown out of joint.

In the middle of the contest the angel asked Jacob what his name was.

Jacob couldn't believe his luck.

Which is why Jacob named that place Peniel which means 'the face of God'.

Jacob's change of name showed that his character had well and truly changed.

Jacob meant 'cheater' but Israel meant 'strives with God'.

The new name of Israel wasn't used much by Jacob but it became the name his descendants used for their new nation.

What Was That All About?

You're probably wondering why on earth an angel would want to have a wrestling match with Jacob on the eve of his return to Canaan.

One of the reasons was that God wanted to see how committed to him he was. Jacob knew that he couldn't be the head of God's nation, the Hebrews, without God's blessing, so he wouldn't let God go until he got it. Not letting go of the angel was Jacob's way of proving that he was going to stick close to God whatever.

Jacob's injured hip would be a constant reminder to him of that special meeting with God.

Fascinating Fact:

Even today the descendants of Jacob don't eat the muscle on any hip-joint.

Esau Isn't Sore

Much to Jacob's utter amazement, Esau was overjoyed to see his long-lost brother.

Only after a lot of persuading did Esau accept Jacob's gifts.
So that was that.
Happy families at last.

Jacob settled here...

and built an altar to God.

It wasn't all plain sailing in Shechem and Jacob's sons had a bit of a bust-up with some of the locals. Well, it was more than just a bust-up. Because one of them had

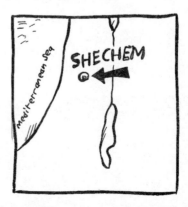

raped their sister, Dinah, they slaughtered the entire family involved. There was nothing for it but to get out of there quick!

GO TO BETHEL AT ONCE AND LIVE THERE.

...said God.

Clean Up The Camp

Jacob realised that if he wanted God to bless them then his family had to get rid of all the idols that they worshipped.
"Purify yourselves and put on clean clothes," ordered Jacob.
Jacob buried all their foreign gods under an oak-tree and set off for Bethel.
The Bible says that a great fear came upon the people of nearby towns as Jacob and his sons began to leave. God was with them and no-one dared stop them.

One More For Rachel

As Jacob and his entourage moved on from Bethel, Rachel gave birth to one more son.
As Benjamin was born, so Rachel died.

"Hi, Dad, I'm Home!"

After years and years of separation Jacob and Isaac were re-united at long last.

Then, at the ripe old age of one 180, as the Bible puts it, Isaac died.

Jacob continued to live in Canaan but now the focus of the story switches to Jacob's sons and in particular someone we've all grown to know and love.

It's none other than that well-known colourful coat-wearer himself...

Joseph!

I'll bet there's someone in your class who's the teacher's pet. It might be great getting special treatment from your teacher but it doesn't do much for your popularity with the rest of the class.

That's what it was like for Joseph.
Not only was he Jacob's favourite son but he couldn't seem to stop himself snitching on his wayward brothers.

There was no doubt about it, Joseph was definitely Jacob's blue-eyed boy.
There aren't many men who are a dab hand at coat-making but Jacob managed to knock together a rather splendid long-sleeved, decorated coat for his favourite son.

Fascinating Fact:

A long-sleeved coat was a sign that the person who wore it would one day be the leader of the family.

Joseph's brothers didn't seem to appreciate Joseph's new piece of clothing. It just showed up their drab working clothes and made them hate Joseph all the more.

It wasn't only Joseph's cloths that got up his brothers noses. Joseph's dreams also made them hot under the collar

Joseph's Dreams - Number One

Some dreams are best kept to yourself especially when the eleven sheaves of corn represented Joseph's brothers and the sheaf in the middle represented Joseph.

Joseph's Dreams - Number Two

This time Joseph told his dad as well as his brothers about the dream.

Even Jacob scolded Joseph for such a ridiculous notion.

"Do you think that I, your mother and your eleven brothers are going to bow down to you?" he asked, but Joseph's brothers just got even angrier at his cockiness.

That last dream of Joseph, was the final straw.

One day, while Joseph was out on an errand for his dad, the other brothers plotted to get rid of him once and for all.

Reuben, the eldest, persuaded them to think again.

Reuben hoped to save Joseph's life and then fetch some help.
When Joseph reached the brothers, they couldn't contain their
anger a moment longer.
They ripped off his new coat and threw him into the well
(which, luckily for Joseph, was dry).
As they were congratulating themselves on a job well done,
along came some Ishmaelites headed for Egypt.

They pulled Joseph out of the
well and sold him for twenty
pieces of silver.

By the time Reuben got back to the well, Joseph was nowhere to be found. Reuben tore his clothes in sorrow.

Meanwhile, the rest of them killed a goat and dipped Joseph's coat in the blood.
They took the coat to Jacob with the news that a wild animal had killed Joseph.
Jacob was heartbroken and refused to be comforted.
Those boys are nasty pieces of work, that's what I say.

Fascinating Fact:

The Ishmaelites who bought Joseph were also known as Midianites. They were desert-dwelling descendants of Abraham. The journey they made from Gilead to Egypt was to trade spices that could be used in food and cosmetics.

Here's the route they would have taken...

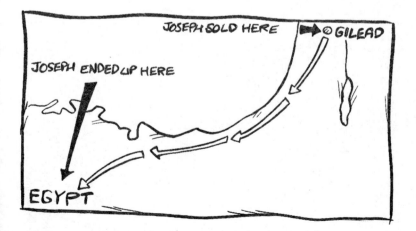

Somewhere In Egypt

On their arrival in Egypt, Joseph was promptly sold to Potiphar, one of the king's officers and the captain of the palace guard.

Let's take a look at what life in Egypt was like...

Potiphar's Potty Wife

Joseph might have been a long way from home but God was still with him.

God saw to it that everything Joseph did was a success.

That meant he was a big hit in Potiphar's household. Potiphar was so pleased with how well Joseph was doing he put him charge of everything.

The Dreamboat Dreamer

The Bible says that Joseph was handsome and well-built.
It also says that Joseph had been noticed by Potiphar's wife!
She had Joseph well and truly in her sights.

When she tried to seduce him, Joseph refused her.
But Potiphar's wife was nothing if not persistent.
Day after day she tried to tempt him but still Joseph said no.
There was no way he was going to betray the trust of Potiphar
but he also didn't want to do anything wrong in God's eyes.

The Key To Joseph's Success

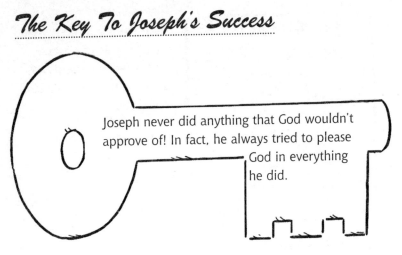

Joseph never did anything that God wouldn't approve of! In fact, he always tried to please God in everything he did.

Potiphar's wife wasn't going to be put off that easily.
One day, when Joseph was all alone in the house she tried one
more time to seduce him.
Once again, Joseph said no but this time Potiphar's wife
grabbed his robe as Joseph made a run for it.
(Joseph doesn't seem to have much luck with coats, does he?)
Not to be outsmarted, Potiphar's wife called to her servants and
pretended that Joseph had tried to rape her and his robe had
been left as he'd made his escape.
Potiphar believed his wife's story and had our hero flung into
prison.

Down But Not Out

Just because Joe was locked up didn't mean that God had forgotten all about him. Joseph had so impressed the jailer that Joseph was put in charge of all the other prisoners and the day to day running of the prison. The Bible says that God blessed Joseph in everything he did.

Lock 'Em Up!

Life in prison was seldom boring. There were always new prisoners being sent down to break the monotony. Two such people were none other than Pharaoh's wine steward and his chief baker.

The Bible says that Pharaoh was angry with them. Perhaps they spilled his drink or cut his bread too thick. Who knows? Whatever they did must have been pretty serious. They spent a long time locked up.

Joseph got given the job of being their servant.

A Good Dream And A Not-So-Good Dream

One night, the wine steward and the baker both had unusual dreams.

...asked Joseph the next morning.

And what about the baker?

Oh dear, it doesn't look like Joseph's smiling...

Unfortunately, it's not going to be such a happy ending for the baker.

Sure enough, three days later, Pharaoh threw a party to
celebrate his birthday. Just like Joseph said, he restored the wine
steward to his former position and had the baker executed.
What's wrong with having an entertainer and some party bags
like the rest of us do?

Why not have a go at saying this all in one breath?
**"What does a young man from the land of Canaan who's
been wrongfully arrested (whilst faithfully serving his
master, Potiphar) and then thrown into prison in a foreign
land because of something he very definitely hasn't done
but is then given the responsibilty for looking after the
other prisoners, two of whom were Pharaoh's wine steward
and his baker whose dreams he correctly interprets thanks
to the ability that God has given him but then still stays
locked up whilst one of them gets released even though the
other one ends up losing his head, do to pass the time?"**

Bet you thought that was a very long sentence, didn't you?
But not as long as the one that Joseph had to serve.
Even though he wasn't guilty of any crime he still had to spend
another two years stuck in jail.

I wonder how Joseph passed the time?

Two years later...

We haven't got long to wait...

Pharaoh wasn't used to having such strange dreams so he summoned his wise men and magicians to tell him what on earth they meant.

Out of the blue, the Pharaoh's wine steward suddenly remembered Joseph and his ability to interpret dreams.

But first...

Fascinating Fact:

To appear before Pharaoh's court you had to be clean-shaven and dressed in linen.

Pharaoh explained his dreams to Joseph and then Joseph explained to Pharaoh that he could only interpret dreams if God showed him their meaning.

Fortunately for Pharaoh (and Joseph) God did.

THEY BOTH MEAN THE SAME THING. THERE WILL BE SEVEN YEARS OF PLENTY IN THE LAND FOLLOWED BY SEVEN YEARS OF FAMINE. YOU NEED TO CHOOSE A MAN WITH WISDOM AND INSIGHT AND PUT HIM IN CHARGE OF THE WHOLE COUNTRY. TAKE A FIFTH OF THE CROPS DURING THE SEVEN GOOD YEARS AND COLLECT IT TOGETHER. WHEN THE FAMINE COMES THE RESERVE SUPPLY OF FOOD WILL KEEP THE PEOPLE OF EGYPT FROM STARVING.

Didn't He Do Well?

Pharaoh and his officials accepted Joseph's interpretation of the dream and also approved of his plans.

HE'S GOOD ISN'T HE?

In fact, our Joe got the top job.
One minute he's banged up in prison and the next he's Pharaoh's number two.
Nice one, Joseph!
Joseph's official title was Governor over all of Egypt.
The Pharaoh removed his engraved ring with its royal seal from his finger and gave it to Joseph. That was Joseph's 'badge' of authority.
He also put a fine linen robe on him and a gold chain around his neck as a reward for his services.

Joseph even got a company car with the job.
Well actually it was a chariot, the second royal chariot!
Wherever Joseph went, his guard of honour cried out, "Make way! Make way!"

And, last but not least, Pharaoh threw in a wife as part of the deal.
Not bad for just interpreting a couple of dreams!

Joseph had served as a slave in Egypt for thirteen years and now at the age of 30 he was promoted to the lofty position of Pharaoh's vizier.

Boring Bible Joke:
Why did Joseph stop drinking water and start drinking coke?
Because coke's a *VIZIER* drink!

Just as Joseph predicted, Egypt enjoyed seven years of plenty.
Every city collected food in vast storehouses.
As sure as night follows day, so the famine that Joseph predicted hit Egypt.
As the famine took hold people cried to their Pharaoh for food and he promptly directed them to Joseph.

It wasn't only Egypt that was affected by the famine.
The terrible famine struck far and wide.
Even in Canaan, Joseph's long-lost family were suffering from its effects.

News reached Jacob that there was corn in Egypt.

Fearing that they would all starve, Jacob sent Joseph's ten half-brothers to Egypt to buy food.

I'M ONE OF JOSEPH'S HALF-BROTHERS!

Benjamin he kept at home for fear some harm might befall him.
He was the only other son that his beloved wife Rachel had given Jacob and thinking that Joseph was dead, he didn't want to lose Benjamin as well.

We Meet Again

Joseph hadn't seen his brothers for over twenty years but when they showed up in Egypt to buy corn he instantly recognised them.
Not knowing who he was they bowed down before him with their faces to the ground.
(Remember Joseph's first dream about his brothers bowing down to him as sheaves of corn?)
Why didn't they recognise Joseph?

BEFORE | AFTER

Probably because he looked so different dressed in Egyptian clothes, clean-shaven and with an Egyptian 'haircut'.

It looks like Joseph's not going to let on who he is yet. I think he's putting them through some sort of test to see whether they've changed after all these years and feel sorry for the way they treated him.

First off, Joseph had them put in prison for three days and then...

Joseph sent them back to Canaan with food and had Simeon tied up and thrown into prison.

The brothers were beginning to suspect that this was punishment for the harsh way they'd treated Joseph.

They were even more worried when, as they travelled back laden with corn from Egypt, they discovered that the money they had taken with them to pay for the corn was back in their bags. (Joseph had returned it but the brothers feared that it might look like they hadn't paid for their corn.)

On their return to Canaan the brothers told their father all that had happened. They greatly feared the governor of Egypt which made Jacob reluctant to let Benjamin, the youngest son, go back to Egypt with them.

After much heart-searching he agreed. It was either that or starve.

Back To Egypt

Joseph still wasn't going to let on that he knew who they were even though they'd brought Benjamin with them. Joseph ordered that his brothers dine with him. The brothers were scared stiff.

It was all Joseph could do to stop himself weeping with joy at seeing his younger brother but he held it all in. By the end of the meal the brothers were drunk.

Joseph got one of his servants to hide a silver cup in Benjamin's belongings.

Next day, Joseph accused the brothers of stealing it.

As a punishment Joseph said he would keep Benjamin as a slave.

The brothers were distraught.

They pleaded with Joseph for mercy.

All Will Be Revealed

When Joseph could bear it no longer, he told his brothers who he was.

Were they overjoyed?...

Joseph did nothing of this sort...

Joseph sent his brothers back to Canaan to get Jacob and all their family and flocks and bring them back to Egypt until the famine was over.

Joseph hugged his brother Benjamin with joy.

And so Jacob came to Egypt and was reunited with his son Joseph.

Jacob and his family settled in the region of Goshen where he lived out his days until he died at the age 147.

The Hebrew people stayed much, much longer in Egypt than they had planned but that's another story. If you want to find out what happened next you'll have to read Boring Bible book *Magnificent Moses* to find out what did become of Jacob and his descendants.

The Bit at the End

Here's some reminders of some of the stuff we've had a look at in *Hotchpotch Hebrews*.

What's Been Happening?

God told Abram to go to Canaan to start a new nation.

Abram and Lot go their separate ways.

God promises Abram an heir (even though his wife can't have kids).

God changes Abram's name to Abraham.

God destroys Sodom (the whole lot...except for Lot!).

Abraham jumps the gun and has a son, Ishmael, by his slave-girl.

Abraham becomes a dad at 100!

Isaac nearly gets barbequed.

Isaac marries Rebecca.

Jacob and Esau, the terrible twins, are born.

Jacob tricks Esau out of his inheritance.

Jacob runs away and marries two of his uncle Laban's daughters.

Jacob does well for himself.

Jacob and family do a runner.

Jacob patches things up with Esau.

Jacob's favourite boy, Joseph, gets a bit carried away (to Egypt, actually).

Jacob interprets some dreams and gets promoted.

Joseph is reunited with his family.

The Hebrews settle in Egypt.

A Quick Run-Down Of The Main Characters

Abraham (was Abram).

Lot.

Quite a few angels.

Sarah (was Sarai).

Hagar and Ishmael.

Isaac.

Jacob.

Esau.

Laban, Leah and Rachel.

Lots of sheep, goats and cattle.

Jacobs twelve sons (I won't bother to name them all again but Joseph is our main man).

Your Turn

Write down any bits of the Bible that you don't think are quite so boring any more...

Don't forget, it's a good idea to have a look at a proper Bible to check out all the stuff we couldn't fit into this Boring Bible book. There are heaps of brill versions that are specially designed for kids!

Have fun!

HERE ARE SOME BITESIZE -BITS- OF THE BIBLE

(JUST TO GIVE YOU A TASTE OF A **REAL** BIBLE!)

GO ON - HAVE A NIBBLE!

The Lord said to Abram, "Leave your native land, your relatives and your father's home, and go to a country that I am going to show you. I will give you many descendants, and they will become a great nation. I will bless you and make your name famous, so that you will be a blessing."

Genesis 12: 1 - 2

'CHEW!

'SLURP!

When Abram was 99 years old the Lord appeared to him and said, "I am the Almighty God. Obey me and do what is right."

Genesis 17: 1

CHOMP!

NIBBLE!

MUNCH!

"I am the Lord, the God of Abraham and Isaac," he said.

"I will give to you and to your descendants this land on which you are lying. They will be as numerous as the specks of dust on the earth."

Genesis 28: 13 - 14

MUNCH!

CHOMP!

CHEW!

So Jacob said to his family and to all who were with him, "Get rid of the foreign gods that you have; purify yourselves and put on clean clothes. We are going to leave here and go to Bethel, where I will build an altar to the God who helped me in the time of my trouble and who has been with me everywhere I have gone."

Genesis 35: 2 - 3

NIBBLE!

SLURP!

When Jacob returned from Mesopotamia, God appeared to him again and blessed him. God said to him, "Your name is Jacob, but from now on it will be Israel."

Genesis 35: 9-10

Now the Ishmaelites had taken Joseph to Egypt and sold him to Potiphar, one of the king's officers, who was the captain of the palace guard. The Lord was with Joseph and made him successful.

Genesis 39: 1 - 2

NIBBLE!

CHEW!

SLURP!

"We will never find a man better than Joseph, a man who has God's spirit in him."

Genesis 41: 38

CHOMP!

MUNCH!

CHEW!

"I am God, the God of your father," he said. "Do not be afraid to go to Egypt; I will make your descendants a great nation there. I will go with you to Egypt, and I will bring your descendants back to this land."

Genesis 46: 3 - 4

SLURP!

NIBBLE!

MUNCH!

"May the God whom my fathers Abraham and Isaac served bless these boys! May God, who has led me to this very day, bless them! May the angel, who has rescued me from all harm, bless them! May my name and the name of my fathers Abraham and Isaac live on through these boys! May they have many children, many descendants!"

Genesis 48: 15 - 16

CHOMP!

CHEW!

MUNCH!

But Joseph said to them, "Don't be afraid; I can't put myself in the place of God. You plotted evil against me, but God turned it into good..."

Genesis 50: 20

'CHEW!

,NIBBLE!

'SLURP!